Nature's Children

DONKEYS

by Dan Doyle

Grolier Educational

FACTS IN BRIEF

Classification of the donkey

Class:	*Mammalia* (mammals)
Order:	*Perissodactyla* (odd-toed hoofed animals)
Family:	*Equidae* (horses)
Genus:	*Equus*
Subgenus:	*Asinus* (asses)
Species:	*Equus africanus* (African wild asses)
Subspecies:	*Equus africanus africanus* (Nubian wild ass; a donkey ancestor) *Equus atlanticus atlanticus* (North African wild ass; a donkey ancestor) *Equus somalicus somalicus* (Somali wild ass)

World Distribution. North and central Africa in the wild. Domestically throughout the world.

Habitat. Desert climates on the North African plains and mountains.

Distinctive physical characteristics. Horselike in appearance though smaller and sturdier with long, upright ears and a tufted tail. Often gray but vary widely in color, with a commonly occurring shoulder-cross made by intersecting stripes on its back and shoulders.

Habits. Live in herds of ten to fifteen in the wild and forage for food during the daylight hours.

Diet. Sparse desert vegetation in the wild. Grass, hay, oats, bran, and corn in captivity.

Library of Congress Cataloging-in-Publication Data

Doyle, Dan, 1961-
    Donkeys / Dan Doyle.
        p.   cm. — (Nature's children)
    Includes index.
    Summary: Describes the physical characteristics, behavior
distribution, and care of donkeys.
    ISBN 0-7172-9118-9 (hardbound)
    1. Donkeys—Juvenile literature.   [1. Donkeys.]   I. Title.
II. Series.
SF361.D69   1997
636.2'82—dc21

97-5976
CIP
AC

This library reinforced edition was published in 1997 exclusively by:

 Grolier Educational
Sherman Turnpike, Danbury, Connecticut 06816

Set ISBN 0-7172-7661-9
Donkeys ISBN 0-7172-9118-9

Contents

2

*Donkeys, like this one in Greece, have served
people for thousands of years.*

Donkeys were among the last animals ever domesticated, or tamed, by humans. At first donkeys were used mainly as livestock, supplying farmers with meat for food, milk for drinking, and skins for leather.

It did not take long, however, before humans realized that the donkey's true value lay elsewhere. This sturdy animal quickly proved that it had great strength and intelligence. As a result, the donkey soon was taking over much of the heavy work on ancient farms.

The sure-footed donkey also became a pack animal, carrying people and their belongings from place to place all around the ancient world.

The donkey is still a hard-working laborer today. In many parts of the world donkeys can be seen plowing fields, pulling wagons and carts, and carrying heavy loads across deserts and over mountain trails.

In recent years, though, donkeys have even found new careers for themselves as pets. And no wonder. With their gentle nature and amusing ways, few creatures are as lovable as the humble donkey.

Part of the Family

Donkeys belong to a family of mammals called equines. Other members of the equine family include horses, zebras, and the wild ass.

The members of the equine family all resemble each other a bit in size and shape. But there also are some obvious differences. The most obvious of these are the black and white stripes of the zebra. Less noticeable is the fact that donkeys are smaller and sturdier than other equines. Another difference is the sounds they make, which range from the donkey's "hee-haw" to the horse's "neigh."

Physically, donkeys weigh between 400 and 600 pounds (180 and 270 kilograms) and stand about 44 inches (1.12 meters) tall. They also have long, upright ears, an upright mane, and large, intelligent-looking eyes. Their tails look like the tufted tails of cows. Most donkeys also have what is known as a shoulder-cross. This is a dark stripe running down their backs and across their shoulders. Most donkeys are gray in color, but because of selective breeding donkeys may be anything from white to black.

Donkeys are members of the equine family, which also includes horses and zebras.

Long Ago and Not So Far Away

About six million years ago, long before there were donkeys, an animal something like the horse developed. Called pliohippus, it stood only four feet (1.2 meters) tall at the shoulders and lived in North America. Eventually pliohippus made its way to Asia, crossing over the land bridge that once connected Alaska to Siberia.

During the next several million years pliohippus spread through Asia and into Africa, where it did extremely well. Somehow, however, pliohippus died out in North America, leaving North America without horses and horselike creatures until Europeans brought them in the late 1400s. But in the meantime pliohippus was doing well in other parts of the world, and from it grew the whole equine family.

As early as 6000 BC people were hunting wild asses—relatives of today's donkey—for their meat. And by 4000 BC people in the Nile River valley of ancient Egypt were domesticating these animals, taming them and raising them for their meat, milk, and skins.

Even today there are donkeys living in the wild.

The African Wild Ass

The domestic donkey of today and the wild asses tamed thousands of years ago are both descendants of the same animal, the African wild ass. Giant herds of these ancient animals once ranged the vast, dry deserts of northern Africa.

Over the years two subspecies of the African wild ass—the Nubian and the North African—developed. It was the Nubian ass that was first tamed and put to use in the Nile Valley.

Eventually these two subspecies bred together. The result was a new breed—a hybrid, as scientists call an animal that results from crossing two species or subspecies. This hybrid became the domestic donkey.

In time a third subspecies, the Somali wild ass, also developed. Unlike the Nubian and North African animals, the Somali has managed to survive in the wild into the present day. But like the others, this creature is facing hard times. In fact, it is now threatened with extinction.

The modern donkey is usually a tame creature, even though its ancestors once roamed wild and free.

The Asian Wild Ass

Wild asses may have almost disappeared from Africa. But the donkey still has a wild relative living in Asia, the Asian wild ass. One variety of this creature is found in the deserts of Mongolia, in central Asia. Another lives in the high valleys in the Himalayas, where it grows a thick coat for protection against the icy mountain cold.

Strangely, although the African and Asian wild asses are very similar in appearance, they really are not very closely related. These two members of the equine family went their separate ways in prehistoric times, and they seem not to have mingled since. Because of this there are important differences between the two creatures.

In the first place, the Asian ass is much more like a horse than the African animal. It even has a voice more like a horse's neigh than a donkey's bray. It also is closer to the horse in size—and in speed. Asian wild asses actually have been clocked at speeds of nearly 40 miles per hour (64.4 kilometers per hour), which makes them nearly as fast as a modern thoroughbred racehorse. But unlike a thoroughbred, the Asian wild ass has the strength to gallop at such speeds for miles and miles.

*Donkeys—even young or slow ones—
usually enjoy a good run.*

A Hard Life

Regardless of where it lived, the wild ass had a hard life. It had a quieter temperament than horses and zebras. It also was smaller in size and, except for a few of the swift Asian wild asses, slower in speed. Because of this it often lost the battle for the best grazing areas and was pushed into the hot, dry deserts.

In time the wild asses learned to survive in these harsh areas. Here their large ears and excellent sense of smell helped warn them of predators. And their strong legs carried them up hills and over rocks when they needed to escape.

In these areas the wild ass's thin coat helped keep it cool, and its large nostrils helped it take in plenty of oxygen, even in the heat of the desert. The wild ass managed, as well, to grow and stay healthy on a diet of brush and hard grass. It also adapted to life with little in the way of water.

These and other adaptations were passed down to the modern descendant of the wild ass, the donkey. They helped it become one of the hardiest animals ever kept by humans.

Today, just as long ago, wild donkeys live in harsh, difficult areas.

Laughing It Up . . . And Other Tall Tales

"Hee haw" is the sound of a donkey's bray, and for some reason people always seem to laugh when they hear it. Perhaps that is because a donkey's bray is such a funny sound. Or perhaps it is because this loud noise comes from such a harmless animal. Whatever the reason, though, people who know donkeys love them for their bray.

Not everything about the donkey is funny, however. The truth is that donkeys definitely have a poor image with the general public. For example, people seem to think that donkeys are rather unintelligent animals. People also believe that donkeys are stubborn. And no one thinks of donkeys as being glamorous, exciting, or romantic, which is how most people usually think of horses.

None of this is true. In fact, according to some experts, donkeys are actually quite intelligent, smarter even than horses and ponies. And donkeys are not really very stubborn either. They simply are cautious and careful when put into new situations.

A Short History Lesson

Just how important has the donkey been to people?
A short walk through history will give you an idea.

More than five thousand years ago, in ancient
Mesopotamia, people of royal blood were so fond of
their donkeys that they asked to be buried with them.
Another great admirer of donkeys was Cleopatra,
the Queen of Egypt in the time of ancient
of Rome. According to many stories, Cleopatra
took baths in donkey's milk. These baths, it was
said, helped her keep her world-famous beauty.

Domestic asses—donkeys—appeared in Europe
around 2000 BC. Donkeys did well in Europe and in
the Middle Ages were more popular for riding than
horses among noble ladies and powerful bishops,
cardinals, and popes. By the 1500s donkeys joined
Spanish sailors and adventurers as they crossed the
Atlantic Ocean to the Americas.

During most of this time these domestic animals
were called by the same name as their wild relatives—
asses. But in the 1700s people began calling them by
the name we know them by today, donkeys.

Donkey or Burro?

For years people in North America, especially the United States, have used the words donkey and burro as if they named two different creatures. In truth, however, the only difference between burros and donkeys is the name. Burro is simply the Spanish word for donkey. But even though it is actually the same animal as a donkey, the burro does have an interesting story of its own.

After Spain conquered the Aztec people in 1521, Spanish settlers began bringing donkeys to Mexico. These donkeys, known as burros to the Spanish, were soon taking part in long journeys into what is now the southwestern United States.

Over the years some of the burros escaped and others were turned loose. These creatures quickly adapted to life in the wild, and they reproduced rapidly. Soon there were many wild burros roaming the dry lands of the Southwest. So in a strange way the burro managed to bring the descendants of pliohippus back to the very land from which it had disappeared thousands of years ago!

The donkey's bray—its famous "hee haw" sound—always seems to make people laugh.

Feral burros are descended from the donkeys brought to Mexico by Spanish explorers and settlers.

Feral Burros

Feral (wild) burros spread through many parts of what is now the southwestern United States. With few natural predators the herds grew. But in time a problem developed that was more than even the hardy burro could handle—human beings.

With poor grazing conditions for either wild animals or livestock, food was scarce in the areas in which the feral burros lived. Water was equally hard to come by. To make room for livestock, ranchers, farmers, and even government employees began "eliminating" the burros, killing them off by the hundreds.

The killing went on for many years. Eventually, however, outraged witnesses spoke up. They organized a nationwide campaign. Even school children helped. Finally in 1971 a U.S. law was passed making it illegal to hunt and kill wild horses and burros.

Today when wild burro populations grow too large, the government holds roundups to gather them together. They are then offered for adoption to people across the country. Since 1971 over 140,000 wild burros and horses have been placed in good homes.

Donkey Diet

Today's donkey does not eat very differently from its wild ancestors. They survived on the thorny bushes and hard grass that most other grazing animals would pass up. Today, even after hundreds of years of life with humans, donkeys can get by on a low-cost diet of grass and hay. No other domestic animal can do so much work in exchange for so little food—and of such poor quality—as the donkey.

For most donkeys the day's meals amount to no more than some grass and hay with small amounts of fresh water. A very well-cared-for donkey will also get a handful of oats, bran, and corn. Oats alone—which horses would love to have—are simply too rich for a donkey's system. The amounts given of this rich food are kept small because the donkey simply will not eat it all at once.

This is not to say that donkeys don't like treats. They have a real affection for vegetable scraps as well as for salt. Owners need to be careful though. Too much food can lead to a fat donkey. And once the weight goes on a donkey, it is hard to take it off.

The fact that donkeys do not need a lot of expensive food makes them especially valuable as work animals.

Caring for Donkeys

Compared to other animals, a donkey's needs are simple. All a donkey really requires is a small stable, a bed of straw, and a door opening out into a garden or pasture.

Donkeys also are almost disease free, which helps owners keep down veterinarian bills. There is little for a vet to do other than give donkeys yearly vaccinations against distemper, influenza, and tetanus. Vets also perform a deworming procedure several times a year.

In general, donkeys do not need the careful brushing, combing, and grooming that horses get. Instead, owners just have to clip donkeys' toenails three times each year.

In the wild donkeys are herd animals, and they are happiest when they are with company. But unlike animals that must have another of their kind around, donkeys will do quite well with some attention from their human owners to make up for the companionship of other donkeys.

Donkeys do not need a lot of care, but like most animals they appreciate love and attention.

Donkeys are so gentle and giving that they actually make good baby-sitters.

Four-Legged Baby-Sitters

In addition to all of their other appealing qualities, donkeys are excellent baby-sitters. First of all, they are alert animals, always watching for trouble. But what makes donkeys truly special is that they will adopt and protect the young of just about any other animal.

Horse breeders, in particular, appreciate these qualities. Donkeys frequently are used as companions for race and show horses. With their quiet temperaments donkeys have a soothing effect on these high-strung, nervous horses.

In addition, young colts often are left with donkeys while they are being weaned, or separated, from their mothers. Donkeys take care of the young horses and cure them of their loneliness. Donkeys are also used to halter-train yearling colts. The two animals are tied together, and wherever the donkey goes the horse learns to follow.

Even more remarkable is the special bond donkeys have with children and people with physical disabilities. This bond often results in lasting friendships. As a result programs have been started in many parts of the world to acquaint such people with donkeys.

Riding

Donkeys are always favorites at children's zoos, amusement parks, and carnivals. Here donkey rides are prime attractions, drawing long lines of happy youngsters. Gentle and easy to ride, the donkeys themselves seem only too willing to let youngsters climb on their backs and go for a slow walk around a ring or corral or even just a walk down a street.

Riders, however, should not expect donkeys to take off like the wind, the way horses sometimes do. Donkeys basically are slower than horses. They may walk or even trot at times. But there is little that can make a donkey break into a full gallop when someone is riding on its back.

Unlike horses—which are known to nip when they are angry—donkeys are gentle even when they are used for riding. They seldom bite, and they almost never turn on their handlers. Once donkeys are sure that the riders or handlers mean them no harm, they will gladly do just about anything they are asked to do.

*Donkey rides are always a popular
activity for youngsters.*

Beast of Burden

Even in an age of machines and technology, donkeys are remarkably useful workers. In fact, they still are a familiar sight at work in certain parts of southern Europe as well as in Asia and Africa, the Middle East, and Central and South America.

Exactly what do the donkeys do? To begin with, donkeys are at home in the kind of rocky, mountainous land that is difficult for even four-wheel-drive vehicles. Scrambling over mountain paths, they can carry goods and materials where almost nothing else can.

In addition there also are areas in which machinery simply won't fit or where people cannot afford expensive, hard-to-operate farm equipment. Tilling the fields in rows of grapes, plowing on steeply sloped land, carrying harvested crops over bumpy farmers' fields, all are jobs for the faithful donkey.

Donkeys are also still in use as pack animals. With their strong backs and gentle nature, they are experts at carrying people and burdens.

Sure-footed donkeys can travel in places no machine could handle—like this trail near the Grand Canyon.

Safe Places

Donkeys may still be in use as workers in many parts of our world. But the days of the donkey's usefulness as a beast of burden clearly are numbered. In more and more places donkeys are being replaced by machines of one kind or another.

As they cease to be useful, donkeys unfortunately end up being mistreated and abused. They also are being abandoned, as people simply turn loose the creatures that once worked so hard for them.

In response to this people have created several organizations to help protect and save the world's donkeys. One of the most important steps has been to create sanctuaries, safe places to which donkeys can be taken to live out their days in peace.

Several of these sanctuaries are in Great Britain and Ireland. The largest, the Donkey Sanctuary, has nine farms set aside for these animals. There almost 7,000 donkeys are kept, animals that otherwise might have continued to be mistreated or even died. Another sanctuary, the Slade Centre, runs an "adopt a donkey" program and gives riding lessons for children with special needs and disabilities.

*Even in an age of trucks and cars
donkeys are useful beasts of burden.*

Breeds

There are many breeds of donkeys, each with its own name and features. But because there are so many breeds, people usually just classify donkeys, regardless of their breed, according to four standards. These standards are size, color, markings, and origin (where that particular variety of donkey was first found). Of these size generally is the most important.

Donkeys are divided into four basic size groups and are measured according to a unit called hands (hh for short). Each hand is four inches (10.2 centimeters), and the animal is measured from the ground to its withers (shoulders).

The first group is miniature donkeys, which are no taller than nine hh (36 inches or 91.4 centimeters). Miniatures include the dwarf donkeys of Sicily and India. These tiny animals stand only six hh (24 inches or 60.9 centimeters) high!

The most common donkeys are Standards, which are between 9 and 12 hh (between 36 and 48 inches or 91.4 and 121.2 centimeters). Large Standards, the third group, are between 12 and 14 hh (between 48 and 56 inches or 121.9 and 142.2 centimeters). The fourth group, Mammoth or Jack Stock donkeys, are over 14 hh (56 inches or 142.2 centimeters) tall. They often reach a height of 16 hh (64 inches or 162.6 centimeters), making them bigger than most horses.

Donkeys range in color from gray to brown to black.

Pedigrees

The price someone pays for a donkey depends on many things. Its size and strength are important. So is its color. Pure black donkeys are rare, for example, and cost more than gray or brown donkeys.

In most parts of the world, however, the price of a donkey depends a great deal on its pedigree. (Pedigree is a term that refers to an animal's ancestors or family tree.) A donkey might have an ancestor that was particularly strong or especially good-natured. This would make the donkey more valuable to someone who wanted an animal with that quality. An animal is even more valuable if one of its ancestors is known to have been a champion.

Donkeys become champions by being judged in competitions. There are several societies that host shows and competitions for donkeys from all over the world. At the shows donkeys are divided according to breeds. Then they are judged by experts who look for such things as a short head, rounded jaws, a long neck, and wide-set eyes.

Donkeys that score high in the competitions win certificates. After a donkey has won a certain number of these awards, it becomes a champion.

How much a donkey costs often depends on its parents' size and ancestry.

Jacks, Jennies, Hinnies, and Mules

What's in a name? When it comes to donkeys, there is a lot. Just like horses, donkeys have special names. A female donkey, for example, is called a jennet or a jenny. A male is a jack. Newborn donkeys have their own name too. They are called foals.

There are two other names associated with donkeys, hinnies and mules. For many reasons breeders have long crossbred horses and donkeys. Sometimes they did this to create an animal that had the physical features of a horse—speed, size, and so on—and the disposition of a donkey. Other times they had different qualities in mind for their crossbreeds, or hybrids.

Just where do the names hinnies and mules fit in? A hinny is an animal that results from crossing a male horse and a female donkey. A mule results from crossing a female horse and a male donkey.

The mule has long been one of the strongest and most valued farm animals.

The Faithful Mule

Although both hinnies and mules have been raised by humans for centuries, mules are by far the better known animal. In some places mules actually replaced donkeys as the work animal of choice. The reason for this is an interesting chapter in the history of donkeys.

As a rule, hybrids have several unusual qualities. One of them is that they usually are sterile, which means that they are unable to reproduce. Another is what is known as hybrid vigor. This means that the offspring of crossbred plants and animals are often larger, stronger, and hardier than either of their parents.

This was one of the main reasons for crossbreeding horses and donkeys. Again and again the hybrids that resulted from crossbreeding these animals were creatures that looked and acted like donkeys but were larger, stronger, and faster than horses.

On top of this, mules are amazingly healthy. They are so healthy that folktales used to say that it actually was impossible for them to get sick. Experts have found that this is not true. But still they seem to be spared many diseases that affect other members of the equine family.

Mating

The animal kingdom has almost always favored the strong over the weak, particularly when it comes to finding a mate. Like many other animals, jacks will fight each other for the right to choose whichever mate they want. The battle is, on one hand, for the right to mate with a jenny. But it is also for power and position within the herd.

Fighting like this, however, seldom happens in captivity. First of all, domestic donkeys are rarely kept in herds. Beyond this breeders simply cannot risk letting any harm come to the jacks they use for breeding. Instead breeders control the process of mating. This saves wear and tear on the jacks. It also allows the breeders to choose the mates that will produce the healthiest and strongest foals.

It takes a full year before a young donkey is born.

Pregnancy

Jennets are pregnant for an entire year before a foal is born. Strangely, during most of this time almost no signs of pregnancy can be seen. Not until the very end of the time do jennets' bodies balloon and sag with the weight of the unborn foals.

Throughout their pregnancy the jennets remain active. In fact, they need almost no extra care at all. The most breeders need to do is to provide a little more food and water and make sure that the stables are dry and free from chilly drafts.

As the time for the foal to be born approaches, a pregnant jennet usually is confined to the stable. Once this is done, the jennet takes care of just about everything else. Surprisingly, it usually isn't necessary for either humans or other donkeys to be around when the birth takes place.

Birth

When it is time for the foal to be born, the jennet usually lies down. Sometimes, though, she remains on her feet and gives birth standing up.

In time the foal appears. The mother helps it out into the world, taking care that the foal is not hurt or scratched in any way. The actual size and weight of a foal depend on the size and weight of its parents. But newborn foals average a weight of 30 to 40 pounds (13.5 to 18 kilograms) and height of 6 hh (24 inches or 60.9 centimeters).

After the birth the new mother completely cleans her foal. Then she gently nudges the baby to its feet. Within an hour the youngster is able to walk.

Donkeys grow faster than horses, but it still takes quite a while before they are ready to live on their own.

Growth and Early Years

Like other animals, foals love to run and play with each other. These games are a way for them to test the speed and agility that once helped them survive in the wild. Now running is simply high spirits and strengthening for the work that may lay ahead.

Donkeys grow faster than horses and ponies. They also do not need as expensive and rich a diet. After just four months young donkeys are fully weaned, which means that they no longer rely on their mothers' milk for their nutrition. By this time they begin to graze on grass, just like their parents.

After one year jacks are separated into two groups, those that are going to be used for "stud" (meaning to breed new donkeys) and those that are not. The animals that will not be fathering foals are then gelded, or neutered, so that they cannot make females pregnant.

A well-kept, happy donkey lives a long life. Some breeds can live to 40 years of age. Given just how useful and gentle these creatures are, it is a good thing for humans that donkeys live so long!

Words to Know

Bray   The donkey's "hee-haw" voice.

Breeder   A person who breeds and raises donkeys.

Colt   A young male donkey.

Crossbreeding   Mating animals of the same family but different species.

Equine   A member of the horse, ass, and zebra family.

Feral   Domestic donkeys that have gone back to living in the wild.

Foal   Donkey offspring less than a year old.

Gelding   A neutered jack donkey.

Hand   A unit of measurement 4 inches (10.2 centimeters) high and abbreviated hh.

Hinny   The offspring of a female donkey and a male horse.

Hybrid   The result of breeding between species.

Jack   A male donkey.

Jennet   A female donkey (also called a jenny).

Mule   Offspring of a jack donkey and a mare horse.

Withers   A donkey's or horse's shoulders.

INDEX

Cover Photo: Wildlife Conservation Society
Photo Credits: The American Donkey and Mule Society, page 18; Kathi Corder (Unicorn Stock Photos), page 20; D. Robert Franz (The Wildlife Collection), page 39; Rod Furgason (Unicorn Stock Photos), page 31; Robert W. Ginn (Unicorn Stock Photos), page 9; Shirley Haley (Top Shots), pages 13, 42, 45; Jean Higgins (Unicorn Stock Photos), page 4; Martin R. Jon (Unicorn Stock Photos), page 11; Marcia Pennington (Unicorn Stock Photos), page 33; A. Ramey (Unicorn Stock Photos), page 29; Ted Rose (Unicorn Stock Photos), page 6; SuperStock, pages 15, 22, 34, 37; Wildlife Conservation Society, pages 25, 26.